DE HAVILLAND
CANADA

This 1960s line-up in front of the Downsview factory of de Havilland Canada shows the Cirrus Moth, G-CAUA in the foreground and behind, from left to right, a DHC-3 Otter on amphibious floats, a US Army DHC-4 Caribou and a DHC-2 Beaver.

DE HAVILLAND CANADA

Rod Simpson

TEMPUS

First published 2002
Copyright © Rod Simpson, 2002

Tempus Publishing Limited
The Mill, Brimscombe Port,
Stroud, Gloucestershire, GL5 2QG
www.tempus-publishing.com

ISBN 0 7524 2126 3

Typesetting and origination by
Tempus Publishing Limited
Printed in Great Britain by
Midway Colour Print, Wiltshire

For operations in remote and inhospitable locations, de Havilland Canada's aircraft are unsur-passed. Here in the foreground is one of a series of Twin Otters used by the British Antarctic Survey and behind it a Turbo Beaver (believed to be VP-FAK – see also page 59) in the bright red colours needed for maximum visibility.

Contents

Acknowledgements   6

Introduction   7

1.   Remote Challenges   15

2.   Training For Peace   33

3.   Working Aircraft   51

4.   Heavy Utility   73

5.   The New Commuter Market   93

6.   Regional Aircraft   111

Acknowledgements

De Havilland Canada has contributed its highly individualistic style to the aviation community for more than seventy years and many aviators have reason to thank the company, its engineers and its workers for their contribution. There are the pilots who gained their skills as they learned to fly in Chipmunks, there are the bush pilots who earned their living at the controls of a Beaver or Otter and there are also the many customers who enjoyed the lifeline which these aircraft provided in the remote areas of the world. In war zones such as Korea and Vietnam the Beaver, Otter and Caribou played an unglamorous role, yet one without which the United States Army's operations would have collapsed. For the businessman in the pinstripe suit, the Twin Otter, Dash-7 and Dash-8 have brought convenient and comfortable transport between meetings. In short, the work of this remarkable company has made a major contribution to society and it is a pleasure to be able to pay tribute to the de Havilland (and now Bombardier) team.

The photographs that illustrate this book have been collected from many sources including the official archives of the company. The origins of some illustrations are unknown, and I apologise to any photographers whose work is included but not acknowledged here. While many pictures are from my own collection and have been taken at various locations around the globe I am particularly grateful to Michael Hooks and Michael Stroud for digging into their collections to find pictures to enrich the book. Specific photo credits are as follows and my thanks go out to those who have been good enough to provide this album recording the activities of a remarkable company. Photos are identified by page number with 'T' denoting the top picture, 'M' the middle and 'B' the bottom picture in each case. Air-Britain: 56T, 64T, Joop Gerritsma: 27B, 287, J.J. Halley Collection: 307, 30B, 31T, Michael Hooks Collection: 4B, 6B, 12B, 17T, 18B, 19T, 20B, 22T, 22B, 23T, 24T, 24B, 25T, 25B, 28B, 29T, 29B, 34T, 34B, 37B, 40T, 40B, 427, 52M, 55M, 55B, 56B, 57B, 59T, 60T, 61T, 627, 62B, 63B, 65, 66B, 67B, 68T, 68B, 73B, 74T, 74B, 80B, 81T, 82B, 84B, 85B, 87T, 87B, 89T, 89B, 90T, 92B, 98B, 100T, 104B, 106B, 107M, 110B, Kenmore Air: 60B, 717, Kansas Aviation Museum (Harold G. Martin archive): 91T Michael Stroud Collection: 2B, 8B, 15B, 16T, 16B, 1ST, 19B, 20T, 21T, 23B, 27T.

Rod Simpson, 2002.

Introduction

By the late 1920s civil aviation was moving from being a public curiosity to a practical means of transport and recreation. The First World War was the catalyst for technological advances that, in less than ten years, took the aviation world from the nail-biting flight of Blériot across the English Channel to high performance fighters such as the Sopwith Camel and SE-5A. The war machine produced talented designers and engineers whose wartime experiences found a new mode of expression in the production of commercial aircraft for peacetime needs – and one of the leading players was Geoffrey de Havilland. He established the de Havilland Aircraft Co. in September 1920 and set up operations at Stag Lane Aerodrome near to Edgeware, north London.

The early de Havilland models were aimed at the emerging public transport market and included such forgotten types as the ten-passenger DH29 Doncaster and also the rather more successful DH34, which was used by Instone Airlines and Daimler Hire. However, wealthy private individuals with a fascination for flying were to become the customers for Geoffrey de Havilland's most successful line of aircraft – the Moths. Following its first flight in 1925, the DH60 Moth took the flying club and private owner market by storm. This tandem two-seat biplane was strong, reliable and affordable. By 1930 de Havilland Aircraft had moved to a new factory at Hatfield and was not only exporting many Moths but also entering into licence production arrangements with companies in other countries including Australia, France, Sweden and Portugal.

Canada was one of the early destinations for new Moths with the Ontario Government acquiring a batch of four Cirrus Moths to act as forest fire spotters. A further order followed, placed in November 1927 by the Canadian Government, for ten aircraft to be used by Canadian flying clubs. Francis St Barbe, then sales director of de Havilland, visited Ottawa in the following month and became sufficiently enthusiastic about prospects for further orders that he quickly recommended that a Canadian branch should be established. Even at this early stage it was clear that there was huge potential for aircraft to be used to give access to the remote settlements of the vast territory. The early sales of Moths were to lay the ground for a unique range of practical utility aircraft that would establish the reputation of de Havilland Canada during the second half of the twentieth century.

The de Havilland Aircraft of Canada Ltd (DHC) was formally constituted in March 1928 under the leadership of Bob Loader who had been charged by the parent company with setting up the new business. A key task was the assembly of the crated Moths that had to be shipped from Stag Lane. The fledgling company started with a wooden assembly building not greatly different from a contemporary portacabin. This was located at Mount Dennis in the north-west corner of Toronto and de Havilland had the use of an adjacent small field for take-offs and landings thanks to the support of the field's owner, Frank Trethewey.

Moths started to emerge from Mount Dennis at the rate of one a week and the little de Havilland biplanes quickly established a reputation that encouraged a healthy flow of new orders and prompted a move to a new factory at Downsview in 1929. Several versions were imported including the DH60 Cirrus Moth with the ADC Cirrus engine, the Genet Moth powered by an Armstrong-

Canadian conditions dictated that de Havilland products would have to work hard in unusual conditions. This early DH60X Moth, G-CAPC, is float-equipped as is the Hatfield-built Giant Moth, G-CAPG, seen on the right.

Siddeley Genet radial and the DH60G and DH60M Gipsy Moths with a final total of 320 aircraft being sold. Other Hatfield-built types supplied in small numbers included the Hawk Moth, Puss Moth, Hornet Moth and the twin-engine Dragon, Dragon Rapide and Dragonfly. Three DH61 Giant Moths were also delivered. These were larger transport biplanes with a fully enclosed main cabin and an open pilot's cockpit in the upper rear fuselage. Two were equipped with large twin metal floats manufactured by Short Bros. Once again, the main role for the Giant Moths was the transport of firefighters within the Province of Ontario.

The summer of 1931 had seen the first flight of de Havilland's most famous biplane trainer – the DH82A Tiger Moth. The fortunes of de Havilland Canada had suffered following the completion of deliveries of Gipsy Moths to the Royal Canadian Air Force and a slackening in demand during the 1930-1933 Depression period. The company was kept alive through a growing overhaul and maintenance business that put it in a good position to embark on manufacturing. In 1937, the RCAF placed an order for twenty-six Tiger Moths that were to be built at the Downsview factory. In the end, over 1,500 Tiger Moths were completed, the large majority being a 'Canadianised' version with a cold weather cockpit and modified undercarriage – and increasing pressure was placed upon DHC to turn out large numbers of these basic trainers as wartime arrived.

Tiger Moths came to be replaced by Mosquitoes and Avro Ansons on the Downsview production line. Wartime employment rose to 7,000 and the factory was continually expanded to fulfil a stream of contracts. May 1945 saw the end of the European war and more than half of the workforce lost their jobs as outstanding contracts were cancelled. Survival for the company meant turning to commercial customers and DHC gradually won contracts to overhaul and refurbish aircraft for civil and military customers around the world. In the early stages there were Catalinas and their Canadian-built version, the Canso, being refurbished for the Danish Air Force, North American T-6 Harvards for the RCAF and a mixture of civil aircraft requiring attention. Manufacturing continued in a small way with licenced production of the DH83C Fox Moth, fifty-three of which were built for Canadian bush operators and private owners. A large contract was obtained for assembly and maintenance of the RCAF's de Havilland Vampire fleet.

Strong in its knowledge of the Tiger Moth, the DHC design team drew up plans for a new all-metal primary trainer. With the moral support of the parent UK company this emerged as the DHC-1 Chipmunk prototype which made its maiden flight on 22 May 1946. It was an elegant little aircraft with enclosed tandem seating and a low wing; it became the RCAF's replacement for the Tiger Moth and was exported to Egypt, India and Thailand. De Havilland Canada completed 217 Chipmunks, but the bulk of production was carried out in England at Chester where 1,014 were built including 740 Chipmunk T10s for the Royal Air Force. A batch of sixty was also produced by OGMA for the Portuguese Air Force. The Canadian Chipmunks differed from their European cousins in having a clear bubble cockpit canopy that afforded better all-round vision than the framed canopy of the Chester-built aircraft.

The discontinuation of Chipmunk production at Downsview in December 1951 was not due to lack of market success but because the next new de Havilland Canada model demanded the production space. The company's understanding of Canadian bush flying had prompted the start of design work in September 1946 on a rugged small utility aircraft that would appeal to both civil and military users. Under Chief Engineer Wsiewolod Jakimiuk, the DHC-2 Beaver was conceived as a no-nonsense single-engined machine with a slab-sided all-metal fuselage, strut-braced high wing and fixed tailwheel undercarriage. Its power plant was the trusty 450hp Pratt & Whitney R-985 Wasp radial that was available in large numbers as war surplus equipment. First flown on 16 August 1946, the Beaver was designed to operate on wheels, floats or skis and the first production aircraft, delivered in April 1948, went to the Ontario Department of Lands and Forests where this capability would be exercised to the full.

The Beaver's success, however, was thanks to the United States Army who conducted a competitive fly-off in December 1950 at Fort Bragg to find a new general utility and liaison aircraft. The Beaver outperformed aircraft such as the Beech Bonanza, Cessna 195, and Aero Commander; by the following November the first production L-20 was being handed over. Orders

The company's first design, the DHC-1 Chipmunk was built in Canada from 1947 but the majority of production examples, such as this RAF aircraft, were built at the parent factory at Hatfield.

from the US. Army and USAF accelerated as the Korean War gained pace and eventually DHC delivered 968 L-20s (later designated U-6) out of a total of 1,632 standard Beavers built between 1947 and 1967. A further sixty aircraft were completed as Turbo Beavers with the Wasp replaced by a 550shp Pratt & Whitney PT6A turboprop. A third of total Beaver production went to civil purchasers and around the world; Beavers became much respected for their strength, performance and reliability. Foreign military users included Peru, Colombia, Chile, Finland, Cuba, Argentina and the British Army Air Corps, and much of the US Army fleet eventually passed into civil hands to start second careers in the remotest parts of the globe.

The Beaver sealed a special relationship with the US Army and it was hardly surprising that they should turn to DHC when they needed more load capacity than the Beaver could offer. The de Havilland design team had launched a new project in 1950 which was initially known as The *King Beaver* and was aimed at existing customers such as the Ontario Lands and Forests who wanted to supplement their fleet of over forty Beavers. Renamed DHC-3 Otter, the new aircraft followed the same high wing layout as the DHC-2 but had a larger fuselage capable of accommodating up to eleven passengers and a more powerful 600hp Pratt & Whitney R1340 engine. Its excellent bush performance was achieved by use of a system of large, slotted flaps connected to drooping ailerons. Such was the pressure on de Havilland Canada to manufacture the Beaver, the Otter and a batch of Grumman CS2F Trackers for the Royal Canadian Navy together with overhaul of a growing number of other aircraft that a brand new factory was built on the south side of Downsview Airfield. This coincided with the twenty-fifth anniversary of the company.

The Otter immediately achieved a respectable order book. Early deliveries were made to the Royal Canadian Air Force who had found the Beaver too small for their needs but progressively received sixty-nine Otters. A further order was received from India whose military forces eventually operated thirty-six aircraft. The US Army was again the largest customer, buying 189 Otters with a further eighteen going to the USAF and US Navy. The Navy aircraft found themselves supporting scientific research teams in Antarctica and established DHC's tradition of providing aircraft which could reliably support the expeditions of several countries. Again,

The success of the DHC-2 Beaver was assured with the award of large US military contracts and many of these aircraft, such as this former US Army example, were subsequently 'civilianised' to become commercial bush planes.

So successful was the Beaver that de Havilland Canada was soon under pressure to build a larger capacity utility aircraft. The DHC-3 Otter not only gained US Army orders but became a sought-after local service airliner for remote operations.

Otters joined commercial operators such as Wardair and Kenmore Air who could accommodate up to ten passengers on low-density services where the Otter's optional floats allowed access to the lakes and coastal waters of North America. In Europe, Wideroes Flyveselskap flew services from fjord to fjord and Qantas used Otters for community services in Papua New Guinea.

During the 1950s, the DHC workforce had grown gradually and after the major cuts of 1945, when Downsview was reduced to almost a skeleton staff, employment had crept up to just over 3,000 in 1960. Overhaul of RCAF Vampires, North Stars and Lancasters had given way to large scale production of the Beaver and Otter and the company was moving forward with another new aircraft – the DHC-4 Caribou – which would take up the space vacated by Tracker production. The Caribou was a significantly larger aircraft than the Otter and, once again, was led by US Army demands for ever-greater tactical supply capacity. The project was initiated in the spring of 1957 and not much more than a year later, on 30 July 1958, there was a prototype in the air. This was DHC's first design with twin-engines, with a retractable tricycle undercarriage and with rear-loading capability – all features that stretched the company's engineering team to the full. In a sense, the DHC-4 was a milestone for the company as it established a new engineering and design pattern that would be repeated in the later Buffalo and Twin Otter and would then lead DHC into the Dash-7 and its current successful commuter airliners – the Dash-8 series.

Orders for the Caribou were slow to arrive, partly as a result of an early crash of the third prototype during its testing period. The US Army was the clear launch prospect but it was not until the late summer of 1959 that the first of their AC-1s was delivered and DHC was already demonstrating the aircraft around the world to drum up orders in case the bulk American military orders failed to materialise. As it turned out, the effort expended on a long series of sales tours paid off with orders for the Caribou from a string of foreign countries which included Australia, Ghana, India, Kenya, Kuwait, Malaysia, Spain and Zambia. The Royal Canadian Air Force also became a

11

Growth in the commuter airline market during the 1960s resulted in large orders for the DHC-6 Twin Otter. These two aircraft for the Bolivian Yacimiento Petroles Fiscales are seen at the Downsview factory prior to delivery in 1973.

customer. Eventually, the US Army received 158 aircraft that proved their worth in the Vietnam conflict. Others were acquired by various units of the Central Intelligence Agency, including Air America, Pacific Architects & Engineers and Bird & Son, who valued the Caribou's short field performance and load carrying ability that was ideal in their clandestine operations.

In some respects, the Caribou was an oddity. At a time when new aircraft were being designed with turboprops, the Caribou was fitted with a pair of Pratt & Whitney R-2000 piston engines. It was inevitable that the follow-on model should be turbine powered and in September 1961 the Caribou prototype was refitted with General Electric T64 turboprops and became the concept prototype for the Caribou II. At the same time, the US Army was looking beyond the Caribou and seeking greater speed and capacity. The result was the DHC-5 Buffalo which resembled the Caribou externally but had a T-tail and a fuselage with greater capacity than that of the earlier aircraft. By the middle of 1965, testing of the Buffalo was complete and the RCAF had placed an initial order for fifteen aircraft. Despite outstanding performance in Vietnam from the evaluation aircraft US Army aviation was in the throes of re-organisation and they failed to procure the Buffalo in substantial quantities. This meant that DHC was back on the road again to maintain the Buffalo production line with foreign military orders and the bulk of production went to Canada, Brazil and Peru. 121 Buffaloes were eventually produced, which was somewhat less than DHC had anticipated.

The Downsview production line was, however, far from empty during the 1960s. The boom in third level airline activity in the United States opened up a market for an economical short range commuter aircraft and DHC responded with an outgrowth of the DHC-3 which was, not surprisingly, dubbed Twin Otter. The DHC-6 had a stretched version of the Otter fuselage, a fixed tricycle undercarriage and a pair of Pratt & Whitney PT6A turboprop engines. It retained the strut-braced high wing and the traditional high lift slotted flaps pioneered in the company's earlier designs gave the Twin Otter the ability to operate from small airfields including downtown 'STOLports'. The prototype flew on 20 May 1965 and Twin Otters started to join small airlines such as Golden West, Air Wisconsin, Pilgrim Airlines and Wardair. As with its predecessors, the Twin Otter regularly operated on floats and skis and was widely acquired by military forces including those of Chile, Ecuador, Argentina and Peru. The initial Twin Otter Series 100 was improved with a lengthened baggage nose and a rear baggage compartment and the Series 300 was re-engined with PT6A-27 engines giving an increase of over 12% in power output. The production line was finally closed in 1988 after 844 aircraft had been completed.

Such was the success of the commuter airline business that greater capacity was required on many of the high demand routes on the American east and west coasts and this led to the development of the DHC-7 'Dash-7' high wing four-turboprop 48-seat airliner. This made its first flight on 27 March 1975. The T-tailed Dash Seven that had STOL capability became much sought after to serve noise-sensitive airports such as London City Airport where it was, initially, the only aircraft able to meet the glideslope and demanding noise standards. Production only totalled 113 aircraft but the majority of these are still in operation and, again, it was widely exported serving with Ransome & Henson Airlines in the United States north-east corridor, Golden West in California and the faithful DHC customer, Rocky Mountain Airways which had a six-aircraft fleet. Overseas, one of the largest users was Arkia which linked the Israeli cities of Tel Aviv, Jerusalem and Eilat. Dash-7s were also sold to Pelita Air Services in Indonesia and Wideroes in Norway.

In some ways, the commuter boom of the 1960s became a victim of its own success. The successful commuter carriers soon became 'Regionals' and moved up to larger aircraft in the Boeing 737 category. Nevertheless, DHC still saw a niche for the modern turboprop airliner. However, orders for the DHC-6 and DHC-7 were tailing off and in 1982 the company announced the new DHC-8 'Dash-8' which would be the basis of a family of airliners to cover a wide range of capacity requirements. NorOntair received the first Dash-8 in October 1984.

By this time DHC and Canadair were both in public ownership through the Canadian Development Investment Corporation but there was a desire for both companies to be privatised

The continuing relationship between DHC and the US Army brought forth the DHC-4 Caribou STOL transport which led to the turboprop DHC-5 Buffalo. This Brazilian Air Force example is typical of many delivered to overseas air forces during the 1970s.

Under the Bombardier banner, DHC is now a leading producer of turboprop regional airliners with its Dash-8 range. This early Dash-8 Series 100 was operated by Talair in Papua New Guinea from 1986 to 1990.

and in January 1986 DHC became the de Havilland Division of Boeing of Canada Ltd. The next four years was an unhappy period in which neither DHC nor Boeing settled down in harmony. Boeing was primarily a 'big aircraft' manufacturer and DHC's 'small' Dash-8s selling at $4 million were small fry compared with even a Boeing 737 selling at nearly ten times the price. Accordingly, negotiations were put in hand again to sell the business and Boeing finally concluded a sale of DHC to Bombardier (51%) and the Province of Ontario (49%). In 1996, Bombardier acquired the Province of Ontario holding and became the full owner of the company.

The initial Dash-8 Series 100 had a maximum of thirty-nine passenger seats but the airframe was designed to be stretched and DHC quickly introduced the Series 300 with up to fifty-six seats. Following NorOntair, many Canadian carriers within the Air Canada and Canadian Pacific groupings acquired the Dash-8 and new aircraft emerged from Downsview in the colours of Air Atlantic, City Express, Air Nova, Air Alliance and Air Ontario. United States regional carriers also acquired the aircraft to fill in on shorter low-density sectors where the MD.80s and 737s were uneconomic and DHC's 500th Dash-8 was delivered to one of the largest users, Seattle-based Horizon Air, in December 1997. The most recent version of the Dash-8 is the Series 400 that is nearly thirty-four feet longer than the original prototype and can accommodate up to seventy-eight passengers. This has entered service with a variety of customers including Lufthansa, SAS and Horizon Air. The Dash-8 range now sits beside Bombardier's highly successful Regional Jets under the Bombardier Regional Aircraft banner and the two classes of aircraft provide a useful operational balance for airlines around the world. It seems probable that de Havilland Canada will have a long and prosperous future within the strong and innovative Bombardier Group.

One
Remote Challenges

The late 1920s saw the fame of the British de Havilland company's Moths spread to Canada where they served initially with the Ontario Provincial Government for forest fire spotting. Such was the commercial opportunity that de Havilland established a Canadian subsidiary, initially to import and service Hatfield-built Moths but later to build a range of de Havilland designs for Canadian customers. During the 1930s, over 400 aircraft came from England ranging from the Cirrus and Gipsy Moth to the Giant Moth, Puss Moth, Dragon Rapide and Dragonfly. As the possibility of war grew the Canadian Government settled on the DH82 Tiger Moth as a new standard primary trainer and the period from 1938 to 1942 saw over 1,500 aircraft built at Downsview – the majority being the DH82C version which was modified to meet Canadian requirements.

De Havilland Canada's factory grew rapidly and became an important production source for both Canadian requirements and for military aircraft needed to fight the battle in Europe. The production lines, which eventually employed 7,000 workers, were turned over from Tiger Moths to the more sophisticated Avro Anson trainers and then to the DH98 Mosquito that continued in production until 1945 when DHC found the opportunity to use its now substantial facilities to build its own original designs.

One of the earliest Moths in Canada was a DH60M, widely flown by Sir James MacBrien, which carried the first of the new CF- registrations, CF-AAA. However, the example shown here is a later DH60G Gipsy Moth, the former G-ABJJ, sold to Canada in 1962 and re-allocated the cherished registration markings.

In 1928, the first home of the new Canadian company was this wooden building at the Mount Dennis Aerodrome near Toronto. It served as an assembly area for new Moths delivered from England. The growth of enthusiasm for the de Havilland products was such that the original assembly shed quickly became inadequate and a move was made to the brand new factory at Downsview seen below. The aircraft is Cirrus Moth, G-CAUA, delivered in August 1928 and now on display at the Rockliffe Museum near Ottawa.

DH60M Moth, CF-OAF was typical of the breed in being fitted with floats for Canadian operations. It is seen here on the water near Toronto Island and appears to be fitted with an oversize
fuel tank on the upper wing centre section.

The DH75 Hawk Moth was one of the less well known designs from the parent de Havilland
company. Of the seven production aircraft, three reached Canada and G-AAFW, seen here on
skis, was delivered initially for governmental use but, once re-registered CF-CCA, was eventually converted into a snowmobile.

The British production line produced three DHG.61 Giant Moths for the Canadian market and G-CAPG is seen here prior to delivery to the Ontario Provincial Services in 1929. It was fitted with large metal floats designed by Short Bros and powered by a Bristol Jupiter radial engine.

The third Giant Moth was CF-OAK; it was built by de Havilland Canada using major airframe assemblies shipped from England. It was unique in being fitted with a 525hp Pratt & Whitney Hornet engine that substantially altered the nose structure of the aircraft.

Another close-up picture of Giant Moth CF-OAK clearly shows the open pilot's cockpit and the enclosed cabin that took up to eight passengers. This aircraft, which was fitted with floats, was used to carry forest fire fighters but sank on landing at Gander Lake in 1936.

CF-AGQ, which was written off in an accident in July 1937, is typical of the thirty-four DHSOA Puss Moths that were imported from England to Canada in the early 1930s. The majority were shipped in component form and assembled at Downsview in the de Havilland Canada factory.

This photo of the Puss Moth CF-PEI (above) clearly shows the large undercarriage support struts which were designed to rotate to face the airflow and act as speed brakes. This particular aircraft is also fitted with outboard leading edge slats. De Havilland introduced the DH87 Hornet Moth in 1935 and ten were shipped from Hatfield and assembled at Downsview. Two, including CF-AYG (below) , were the early DH87A model with pointed wingtips.

De Havilland Canada took on the task of engineering the Hornet Moth for float operation. The twin floats were designed by Fairchild and are seen here fitted to CF-AYJ, a DH87B used by the company's Managing Director, P.C. Garrett.

Another float-equipped Hornet Moth, CF-AYI. It was a DH87B and the squared-off wingtips of the later Hornet Moths are clearly visible, as is the long engine exhaust pipe that was a standard design feature.

Several examples of the DH84 Dragon were sold to Canadian operators and CF-AVD was a Dragon 2 with the modified cabin windows used on the later Rapide. It was operated by Canadian Airways and was finally written off in a take-off accident in May 1944.

The DH89 Dragon Rapide was imported from England in fair numbers and this line-up shows four Rapides of Quebec Airways fitted with their winter ski undercarriages. The airline used them for services between Harrington Harbour and Rimouski.

Canadian Rapides such as CF-BNG were delivered with the modified fins designed for the DH89M military reconnaissance variant. This was necessary to provide the additional side area needed to provide stability when floats were fitted.

The five-seat DH90 Dragonfly was smaller than the Dragon Rapide and was not wholly suitable for Canada's heavy-duty bush flying. Eight were imported into Canada, the first of which was CF-AYF (above), used by Consolidated Mining & Smelting. It was fitted with the standard vertical tail.

One of the Canadian DH90 Dragonflys equipped with skis for winter operations. Note the complicated arrangement of bracing struts to the rear of the skis and the spring-loaded chords in front. All but two of the Dragonflys delivered from the UK to Canada went to the Royal Canadian Mounted Police and carried appropriate registrations and a distinctive blue and yellow colour scheme. They have the extended fins necessary for float operation – although in practice, floats were never actually fitted.

Most of the RCMP Dragonflys served as trainers with the RCAF during the war. One of the survivors was CF-BFF (above), used after the war by Golden Belt Air Services. It was the only Dragonfly to be fitted with Fairchild floats.

In 1937, DHC received its first order for Tiger Moths for the RCAF. The Canadian DH82C differed from the British-built aircraft in several ways and CF-CKW (above) shows the large sliding cockpit canopy fitted to keep out the Canadian winter cold.

Now owned by the Rhinebeck Air Museum, this DH82C Tiger Moth, N8731R, shows the cut-down cockpit sides resulting from the canopy installation and the narrower steel tube inter-plane struts which replaced the broad wooden struts of the British 'Tiger'.

G-ADGV, a Hatfield-built Tiger Moth provides an interesting comparison with the Canadian version. It has a tail-skid whereas the Canadian aircraft had a tailwheel, and the main under-carriage legs of the DH82C were angled forwards to prevent nosing-over accidents.

The modification to the undercarriage of the DH82C Tiger Moth resulted in a lower ground angle as is evident in this shot of CF-FLD. Also seen here is the cut-out step behind the engine cowling to give access to the fuel tank and another step to ease entry to the rear cockpit.

After a long career with the RCAF as 8870, this Canadian Tiger was civilianised as CF-DHR and is seen here in 1982 at a fly-in at Brampton, Ontario.

Tiger Moth C-FCTN was restored with its original RCAF markings and serial 5884. This photo shows the modified cockpit of the Canadian aircraft and the prominent dividing bulkhead between the seats that mounted the instrument panel for the rear occupant.

Another view of a Canadian-built Tiger Moth – in this case CF-COU seen at the Oshkosh Fly-In in 1989. This appears to be a DH82C2 'Menasco Moth' with the shorter engine cowling of the Menasco Pirate 4 engine.

In February 1940, de Havilland Canada started assembly of the Avro Anson I that was needed for the Commonwealth Air Training Plan. One of the first aircraft shipped from England is seen here in front of the Downsview factory.

After assembling 264 war weary Ansons shipped from England, DHC started manufac' Anson II which was powered by Jacob's radial engines in place of the normal Arms Cheetahs. Ansons are seen here waiting for their morning training detail in Canada

1941 saw de Havilland Canada tasked with the manufacture of DH98 Mosquitos. The first three were the FB.21 with Packard Merlin 31 engines but the main production version was the FB.26 with Merlin 33s as exemplified by KB135 seen here.

KA100 was the first of three FB.21s produced and it is seen in Canada prior to its delivery to England. Sadly, it was one of twenty-eight Mosquitos written off in various circumstances during the ferry flights which started in August 1943.

KA888 seen in this picture was a Mosquito T. Mk27 from the Downsview production line. Powered by Packard Merlin 225s, the T.27 was a dual control aircraft with a solid nose and nineteen were completed.

After the war up to 200 Canadian-built Mosquitos were delivered to the Nationalist Chinese Government and the aircraft seen here is the former KA203 – a Mosquito T.29 trainer carrying the distinctive Chinese blue and white twelve-pointed star markings.

After the war, Mosquitos were used as photographic survey aircraft by several operators including Kenting Aviation and Ottawa-based Spartan Air Services. The Spartan Mosquito 35, CF-HMQ, (above) withdrawn from use at Toronto in 1966, was actually a British-built aircraft (ex VP189) delivered to Canada in June 1955. Another Mosquito B.35 intended for survey work with Spartan was CF-IMB (below) pictured at Croydon in 1955 and showing clear evidence of its former RAF markings, VP200, on the rear fuselage. It was one of five aircraft prepared for Spartan but the order was cancelled and they never reached Canada.

Two

Training for Peace

In common with many other manufacturers who had geared up for wartime production, de Havilland Canada had to move quickly to fill their empty production hangars at Downsview. While the American manufacturers over the border in Kansas were starting to turn out large numbers of all-metal light aircraft, DHC set up a small production line to build new Fox Moths. However, the main work in 1946 was the overhaul and refurbishment of a variety of heavy aircraft including Catalinas for Denmark, and Lancasters, Harvards and, later, Vampires for the RCAF. The evident need for a less costly and more broadly based trainer to replace the venerable Harvard resulted in the new DHC-1 Chipmunk that took DHC away from its traditional wood construction methods into modern all-metal monocoque structures. The Chipmunk was quickly adopted by the RCAF who were enthusiastic about its classic handling characteristics. While the RCAF equipped itself with seventy-nine DHC-built Chipmunks, the main success for the design was to come from the parent company in England. They evaluated the prototype Chipmunk at an early stage and put it into production at Hatfield to meet large orders from the Royal Air Force. Chipmunks from the Canadian and British production lines also went to private owners and flying clubs and to many overseas air forces, including those of Saudi Arabia, Ghana, Ireland, Denmark and Thailand. A batch was also built by OGMA in Portugal for the Portuguese Air Force. More than fifty years later, many Chipmunks continue to give excellent and reliable service around the world.

Chipmunk G-AMUF shows off its clean lines in front of Hangar 6 at its home base at Redhill in south-east England. A Hatfield-built Chipmunk, it started its life in 1952 as part of a six aircraft fleet operated by Air Service Training Ltd at Hamble.

De Havilland Canada launched into peacetime production with the DH83 Fox Moth, fifty-three of which were built for Canadian customers and for export to Pakistan, New Zealand and India. They were typically operated on floats and CF-BNR is seen above on the water near Toronto's Island airport. The Fox Moth used Tiger Moth wings and was therefore a very straightforward aircraft for de Havilland Canada to build. This example, CF-DJC (c/n FM.29) (below) was the first aircraft operated from Yellowknife by the well-known aviator, Max Ward, who went on to establish Wardair as a major airline.

DHC built up a thriving business in overhaul of a variety of aircraft types. The Royal Danish Navy received a batch of eight PBY-5A Cansos from this source and the aircraft seen here is one of their later PBY-6As used for patrols around Greenland.

A number of Douglas C-47s underwent major and minor overhaul at Downsview during the early 1950s and seen here is a RCAF example, 662, which later served with the Muscat & Oman Air Force and in Colombia.

The Noorduyn Norseman was a mainstay of the RCAF during the post-war years and many received attention from the hands of de Havilland craftsmen. This RCAF Norseman, serial 790, is seen on skis in the winter of 1946/47.

The Downsview workshops also saw a steady stream of North American T-6 Harvards pass through during 1948 for refurbishment to meet post-war RCAF training requirements.

De Havilland Canada's first original design was the DHC-1 Chipmunk. The prototype CF-DIO-X (above) made its first flight on 22nd May 1946. It was subsequently shipped to England where it became G-AKVE and it was eventually retired in 1951.

The eleventh Canadian-built Chipmunk was also sent to England as G-AKDN and was used by the A&AEE at Boscombe Down for evaluation prior to the Chipmunk being selected as the RAF's new primary trainer. It won the 1953 King's Cup Air Race and remains in active use with a private owner forty-four years after it was built.

The Royal Canadian Air Force received seventy-nine Chipmunks and these differed from the prototypes in having a large sliding blister canopy and no fairings on the undercarriage legs. This example is a Chipmunk T.30 from the main sixty-aircraft batch delivered during 1956.

This bright yellow Chipmunk T.30 started life as 18038 with the RCAF (later renumbered 12038) and was then civilianised as CF-BNB before being sold to an American private owner based at Scottsdale, Arizona.

In total, 217 Chipmunks were built at Downsview and export customers included the Indian Flying Clubs and the Egyptian and Royal Thai Air Forces. Three, including L-106 seen above, were sold to the Lebanese Air Force, supplemented by a further six from the Hatfield production line.

This Canadian Chipmunk (c/n 140-178) was a civil aircraft originally delivered to the Victoria Flying Club as CF-CYJ and later used as a tug by the Saskatoon Soaring Club. It is shown here in natural metal finish and registered N12730 while in use by Spinks Enterprises of Dallas, Texas.

Chipmunks have suffered many engine modifications and one of the earliest was this installation of a 190hp Lycoming 0-435-A in the sixth Chipmunk, CF-DJS-X. It did not offer great improvement over the standard Gipsy Major in-line engine.

Caught on camera at Lethbridge, Alberta is CF-RWC which spent its early years as 18031 training RCAF pilots. It was later sold to the United States and now lives in Texas as N9JD with R.A. Cain.

Until they were ousted by the Pitts Specials and Sukhoi Su-26s, Chipmunks were popular with the American competition acrobatic performers. This much-modified Canadian Chipmunk, N6311V (c/n 137-175), is seen at Reno in 1967 where it was flown into second place in the National Aerobatic Championships by its owner, Harold Krier.

The World Aerobatic Championships in Moscow in 1966 saw this Chipmunk, N13A (c/n 111-149) being flown by the American champion pilot Art Scholl. It has a modified Spinks rudder and a 200hp Ranger engine with a variable pitch propeller.

Another Chipmunk much modified for air show work is N260DC (c/n 180-218), above, seen at Lakeland, Florida in April, 1999, which has another type of enlarged rudder, wingtip end-plates and a streamlined custom engine cowling for its Lycoming engine. Not immediately recognisable as a Chipmunk, N13DW, below, is a British-built machine imported into the USA from Australia by Frank Ryder. It now has a modified tail and a 295hp Lycoming GO-480 engine to provide the power for its air show performances.

The Super Chipmunk is a new copy of the original available to homebuilders as a kit. Its fuselage, which is wider than that of the standard Chipmunk, has a steel tube framework. The prototype, C-GLSC is shown here taxiing at the 2000 Oshkosh AirVenture Fly-ln.

The parent de Havilland company in Britain obtained a large order for Chipmunks for the Royal Air Force. A pair of RAF aircraft, WK582 and WP908, in the early silver and yellow markings, are seen in formation over the English Channel with one of the North American Harvards which they replaced.

The early yellow bands on the RAF Chipmunk T. Mk.10 gave way to day-glo stripes during the 1960s. WP973 of the Edinburgh University Air Squadron wears these markings as it awaits its trainee pilot at Turnhouse Airport in 1963.

The Royal Navy had a small number of Chipmunks including WP856 shown here at Plymouth – Roborough in 1975 where it was used for training officer cadets from the Dartmouth Naval College. The Hatfield-built Chipmunks all had the original framed cockpit canopy and were fitted with anti-spin strakes on the rear fuselage.

The day-glo markings of the 1960s eventually gave way to a new red and white colour scheme for trainers introduced in the early 1970s. WZ856 wears this livery in this 1993 picture when it was in service with 7 Air Experience Flight at Newton.

While the RAF became the largest Chipmunk customer, many aircraft were sold for civil use. G-ALWB started life as the de Havilland demonstrator and won the prestigious Goodycar Trophy Race in 1951. After a spell with the Lebanese Air Force it returned to Britain and now, clad in a smart black and gold colour scheme, is owned by J.M. Soper at Perth in Scotland.

Chipmunks were popular with flying clubs and schools around the world. This aircraft served for a while with the Malay Auxiliary Air Force and then with the Royal Malaysia Air Force prior to being sold to the Kuala Lumpur Flying Club and then the Seletar-based Singapore Flying Club in whose service it is seen here.

Fourteen Hatfield-built Chipmunks were supplied by the British Government to the Ghana Air Force in 1960. This aircraft, G159, was formerly with the RAF as WB554. It was probably written-off during its Ghanaian service as it was not part of the surviving nine Chipmunks declared surplus in 1976.

In Portugal, OGMA opened up a production line and built sixty-six Chipmunks for the Portuguese Air Force. This Chipmunk, 1302, was one of an initial batch of ten aircraft built at Hatfield and in 1989 it was sold to France and became F-AZNE.

Another globetrotting Chipmunk was 9M-ALD seen running its engine during its service with the Kuala Lumpur Flying Club. It was originally a RAF aircraft, WB667, but became G-APAB before export to Singapore and later sale to Malaysia. Today it is one of a large number of Chipmunks based in the USA.

For many years, the Lufthansa pilot training school at Bremen used a fleet of Chipmunks for primary instruction. These were former RAF aircraft made available by the Airways Aero Association. D-EFOL was the former G-AOJP and was written off in an accident at Wilhelmshaven in June, 1964.

The Chipmunk 23 was a conversion of the standard Hatfield-built aircraft for crop spraying. The front cockpit was fitted with a chemical hopper and the rear cockpit was fitted with a new windshield and enclosed canopy to enclose the pilot. G-ATVF, seen here at Sywell, was one of five aircraft so converted.

Bristol Aircraft's Managing Director, Peter Masefield, saw the Chipmunk as an ideal touring aircraft and, in 1956, acquired WP988 from the RAF. As G-AOTM it underwent several improvements including a streamlined engine cowling, clearview cockpit canopy, enlarged windshield and stylish undercarriage spats. Several other Chipmunks experienced the Masefield touring conversion. G-APOY was fitted with a clearview canopy but did not have the stream-lined windshield or engine cowling and was equipped with less complex wheel spats.

In September 1966 this Chipmunk appeared at the Farnborough Air Show to demonstrate a Rover TP-90 light turboprop engine which had been installed by Hants & Sussex Aviation. The aircraft later reverted to the normal engine installation and now flies with a private owner in the USA.

The 1980 Farnborough Air Show saw another Chipmunk, G-ARWB, appearing as a test-bed. Designated Chipmunk 200, it was fitted with Bill Bonner's 230hp water-cooled Super Sapphire V-6 piston engine. It is now back in standard configuration and flies in its original RAF markings as WK611.

Three
Working Aircraft

Pre-war sales of de Havilland aircraft had provided DHC with a solid understanding of the benefits aviation could bring to people in the remote Canadian territories. The post-war quest for new production work to fill the Downsview factory placed a high priority on the obvious market for rugged utility aircraft. Such machines needed to be tough and reliable; they needed to be able to operate on wheels, skis and floats and they needed to cope with extremes of weather without complaint. The de Havilland answer was the DHC-2 Beaver which appeared in August 1947. With its slab-sided fuselage and chunky Pratt & Whitney radial engine the Beaver was practical rather than elegant. However, it achieved all its goals from the start and with no more than minor changes it went into production. This was soon boosted by the award of a large contract from the USAF and US Army who were in need of a 'flying truck' to support the war developing in Korea. The Beaver was soon in demand from commercial operators and military forces all over the globe and 1,692 were eventually built, including sixty examples of the PT6-powered Turbo Beaver. Beavers were used for all types of task including crop spraying, aerial survey and local airline work and good Beavers are still in demand more than fifty years after the type was first introduced.

A familiar and welcome sight to waiting sport fishermen – a Turbo Beaver, N260HC, arrives over a Canadian lake sporting its large amphibious floats.

One of the earliest L-20As (52-6062, c/n 404) to be delivered to the United States Air Force. USAF machines generally retained their natural metal finish while US Army Beavers were painted in olive drab.

Beavers served in Korea and Vietnam and 57-6140 (c/n 1223), right, was one of a batch of U-6As handed over to the South Vietnamese Army and photographed at Tan Son Nhut in 1965.

A handful of Beavers went to the US Navy for special duties and this U-6A, Bu.150191 (formerly designated L-20A) is one of three used by the US Naval Test Pilot's School.

Seen landing at Rotterdam Airport is a Dutch civil Beaver, PH-VTH. It was delivered by DHC to the Delft Vliegtuigbouwkunde in 1958 who used it until April 1997 when it was sold to the USA, becoming N243A.

The Finnish Air Force acquired a pair of float-equipped Beavers, the first of which was BV-1 (c/n 1061) seen in this photo prior to delivery from Downsview. The ventral fin attached to the rear fuselage is noteworthy.

The colourful red, black, green and gold markings of the Kenya Air Force adorn the sides of this Beaver. Eleven Beavers were delivered in 1964 and this aircraft, KAF-102 (c/n 1552) was subsequently sold to the East African Desert Locust Control organisation as 5Y-BCL.

The Colombian Air Force obtained twenty Beavers, the last of which is seen here in a natural metal finish with the country's blue, red and yellow national markings. All of the Colombian Beaver fleet was withdrawn from use in the 1980s.

In 1949, the parent de Havilland Aircraft Co. at Hatfield imported Beaver G-ALOW to act as their sales demonstrator. It remained in service until November 1952 when it was sold to Southern Rhodesia as VP-YKA and later served with Zambia Airways as 9J-RKA. The Beaver 2, below, was an experimental development fitted with an enlarged vertical tail and a 550hp Alvis Leonides engine in place of the normal Pratt & Whitney Wasp Junior. CF-GQE was converted in March 1953 and was later sent to England as G-ANAR for British Army trials. In the event, the Beaver 2 was not put into production despite its superior performance.

In this picture taken at Downsview, the Beaver 2 (G-ANAR, c/n 80) is on the right, fitted with floats and re-registered CF-CNR after its return from England. The longer engine cowling and modified tail can be compared with the standard Beaver on the left.

In Britain, de Havilland was successful in selling the Beaver to the British Army as a light utility transport. Forty-six aircraft, including XP810 (c/n 1464) seen above, were delivered and served with the Army Air Corps from 1961 to 1989.

The British Army batch of Beaver AL.1s included four acquired for the Sultanate of Muscat & Oman. Painted white overall, they wore British serial numbers and the Omani national markings on the wings and tail.

Typical of the many Beavers used by established airlines for remote services is this float-equipped aircraft, VH-EAT (c/n 645), used by Qantas in Papua New Guinea.

Another user of Beavers in remote locations was Wardair who built up a fleet of Beavers and Otters during the early 1950s. This company publicity photo of a ski-equipped aircraft was taken near Kapuskasing in eastern Ontario.

This Beaver, N9762Z (c/n 302), of Kachemak Air Service Inc. shows the additional tail fins fitted at the outer ends of the tailplane for float operations. This Beaver started its life as an L-20A, delivered to the USAF as 51-16517 in June 1952.

The Canadian operator, Baxter Aviation, based at Nanaimo in British Columbia, has a fleet of nine Beavers including C-FEBE, shown here taking off from Vancouver on a scheduled air taxi service across the Strait of Georgia.

Several Beavers were imported into Japan by C. Itoh & Co. who were the local sales agents. This aircraft, JA3111 (c/n 1049), was delivered in July, 1957 and is shown here equipped with skis and in use by the Japanese Antarctic Expedition. It was subsequently sold to Colombia.

New Zealand was another country engaged in Antarctic research and they used this Beaver, NZ6001, painted in a bright red colour scheme with black trim. Adorned with Trans Antarctic Expedition titles, it is now based at Ardmore Airfield in private ownership as ZK-CKH.

Another Antarctic aircraft. This Turbo Beaver C-FCKW was originally delivered for use in the Falkland Islands by the British Antarctic Expedition as VP-FAK.

The DHC-2T Turbo Beaver first flew in 1963 and was powered by a Pratt & Whitney PT6A-6 turboprop engine. In total, sixty new Turbo Beavers were built including this aircraft (EP-RLS, c/n 1614) for the Iranian Red Lion & Sun organisation.

One of the best known operators of the de Havilland Canada bush planes is Kenmore Air of Seattle, Washington who have around twenty aircraft including Turbo Beaver N1455T which is used for taking fishermen and tourists to isolated lakes in the north-western United States and Canada.

Originally called the King Beaver, DHC's DHC-3 Otter built on the undoubted success of the Beaver and the prototype flew in December 1951. The US Army acquired an initial batch of six standard Otters known as YC-137s, three of which are seen here, followed by 184 production examples designated U-1A.

The European-based U-1A Otters of the US Army were painted in an overall olive drab colour scheme with yellow serial numbers. This one, 55-3298, was photographed at Edinburgh-Turnhouse in 1957 and was eventually destroyed in action in Vietnam in January 1971.

Five Otters were ordered by the Chilean Air Force and handed over in 1957. This is the first of the batch that was written off after an accident in November 1966. However, Otters are tough aircraft and the wrecked aircraft was rebuilt and returned to service in Alaska with the Bear Lake Lodge Ltd. Indonesia was the destination for seven Otters, some of which were supplied under the Colombo Aid Plan. The silver painted Otter, seen below, is believed to be ELL-200 (c/n 263) handed over by DHC in June, 1958 although the photo was, presumably, taken at Downsview earlier in the year.

The Royal Canadian Air Force had not ordered Beavers, possibly because they were considered too small, but sixty-nine Otters were ordered and many were used for military and civil emergency rescue duties. This aircraft, 3691, is one of the RCAF Otters delivered in 1954 and was based at Namao, Alberta, Greenwood, Nova Scotia and Trenton, Ontario during its service life.

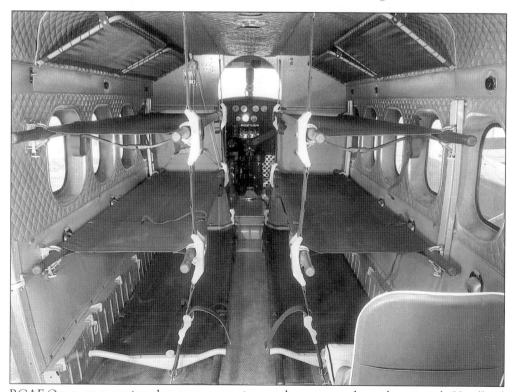

RCAF Otters were equipped to carry up to six stretcher cases as shown here in a de Havilland Canada photo. These Otters were capable of being converted rapidly from passenger to ambulance configuration.

When they started to be released from RCAF service in 1963 the Otters were purchased by various commercial operators. This photo shows 3634, with taped-on ferry markings CF-GTL, prior to delivery to Lambair Ltd.

Ten Otters joined the Royal Norwegian Air Force and No.5331 is shown here in its initial code markings, O-AG. It served in the Antarctic and was subsequently re-coded as XJ-U with 719 Squadron and eventually went to the civil airline operator Wideroes as LN-LMM.

Wardair was a faithful de Havilland Canada customer and they used five aircraft at various times. Their primary task was to transport geologists, oil executives and medical staff to the Arctic bases at Eureka, Mould Bay and Alert Bay.

The Norwegian fjords were natural territory for the Otter and Wideroes Flyveselskap og Polarfly had six green and white Otters on floats which were used for scheduled services between Stavanger, Bergen, Tromso and Bodo. This shot of LN-SUV was taken at Bodo in September 1960.

In Canada, Canadian Pacific Airlines purchased two Otters, CF-CZO and -CZP, to operate feeder services in the Mackenzie District of the North West Territories. They flew twice-weekly services linking Norman Wells, Fort Macpherson, Arctic Red River and Aklavik. In 1959 the routes and aircraft were passed to Pacific Western who eventually operated six Otters.

The US Navy was a relatively small user of Otters but they took delivery of fourteen aircraft. This Otter, 141670, was acquired for Antarctic support work with VX-6 Squadron but was later posted to NAS Patuxent River to join the fleet of the Naval Test Pilots' school where it is seen in this recent picture.

In 1956, the British Commonwealth Trans-Antarctic Expedition obtained Otter XL710 to supplement two small ski-equipped Austers. It made the first non-stop flight across the Antarctic in January 1958. It was later used by the US Navy and the RNZAF before being sold to Georgian Bay Airlines and then being converted as a Turbo Otter.

One of the early production Otters (c/n 17) was handed over in July, 1953 to de Havilland Aircraft in England to become their demonstrator as G-ANCM. Four years later it was sold to the Indian Air Force where it became their first Otter, serialled IM-1057.

The Indian Air Force purchased thirty-six Otters including five released by the RCAF. One of the first to be delivered in 1957 was IM-1708 (c/n 206) and the final aircraft was handed over in 1966. The Otters were used as general-purpose transports and while thirteen, including this one, have been sold to North American civil users, at least ten are thought still to be in Indian service.

A popular improvement to the Otter has been the replacement of the Pratt & Whitney R-1340 engine with a 600hp PZL-3S seven-cylinder radial as seen on CF-KOA of Plummers Lodge. This engine, fitted by Airtech Canada, is lighter and more efficient than the Wasp, giving the Otter improved take-off performance.

This is C-FIFP, another Otter modified by Airtech with the 1,000hp Polish-built ASz-621R power plant. In this form it is known as the DHC-3/1000 and the much shorter engine cowling used on the Airtech conversions is evident in this picture.

C-GKYG of Eagle Aviation is another float-equipped Otter-1000 with the ASz-621R engine. Originally delivered to the US Army in 1958, this Otter was used later by the US Department of the Interior and Winnipeg-based Keewatin Air.

The most popular Otter conversion has been to turboprop power. Here, C-GOFB has been fitted with a Pratt & Whitney Canada PT6A and is seen in Watson's Skyways colours at Lakeland, Florida in 1999.

Kenmore Air, based at the top of Lake Washington, to the north of Seattle, is one of the world's largest commercial users of Beavers and Otters. They have four Turbine Otters including N234KA (c/n 42) which started its career with the Royal Canadian Mounted Police.

Well known for turbine conversions of helicopters and Cessnas, Soloy Corporation has jointly developed its Dual Pac Otter conversion with Pratt & Whitney Canada. The new engine installation combines twin PT6A turbines driving a single propeller as seen here on the test aircraft, N5010Y.

Another Turbine Otter, in this case N888KA of Ketchum Air Service found on the hard standing next to the Lake Hood seaplane base at Anchorage. As with many other hard working Otters this aircraft started as a US Army U-1A and was released to the civil market in August 1978.

Sound Flight, based at Renton, Washington, operates this Turbine Otter, N24SF. In addition to the turboprop engine installation, this Otter has been fitted with enlarged rectangular windows to improve the view for passengers.

Four
Heavy Utility

Spurred by the fruitful relationship built up with the US Army during the Beaver and Otter production programmes, de Havilland Canada conceived a new twin-engined aircraft which would not only offer the rugged dependability of the earlier types but would also have exceptional tactical STOL ability. The DHC-4 Caribou immediately received a US Army order for five YAC-1 evaluation examples, and little more than a year later the prototype flew. Eventually, DHC built 159 production CV-2 Caribous and they served with distinction in the Vietnam War. In the end, 307 Caribous were produced and while they did not have great impact on the commercial sector they were sold to many air forces around the world. The Buffalo that followed was a higher capacity aircraft with more than three times the payload and turboprop engines in place of the Pratt & Whitney R-2000 piston engines of the Caribou. Quantity orders from the US Army for the Buffalo were not forthcoming but de Havilland's reputation won them orders for 120 aircraft from Brazil, Canada, Ecuador and several African airforces. Many of the Caribous and Buffalos have now been retired by their military users and are finding a new life with civilian owners who appreciate their short field performance and ability to lift large loads.

The Ghanaian Air Force purchased a batch of seven DHC-4 Caribous, the second of which is seen here. They remained in service until the mid-1970s at which time they were replaced by Fokker F.27s and this aircraft (c/n 31) was sold in 1979 to the Indian Air Force as M2169.

The de Havilland demonstrator Caribou, CF-LVA (c/n 9), is shown in this picture near to the Downsview factory in late 1960. Clearly visible is the anhedralled wing centre section that allowed the designers to fit a short-stroke undercarriage while retaining the high wing layout. It later became JW9012 with the Tanzanian Air Wing.

As a practical way of concept-testing the Caribou, de Havilland used the prototype Otter fitted with a cradle to carry models of the DHC-4. Various configurations were investigated and the model seen here has a flattened V-tail. The cradle could be adjusted to review performance in a variety of flight attitudes.

The early US Army Caribous were designated CV-2A and the last of the batch of fifty-six aircraft, serialled 61-2600 and painted in European standard olive drab overall camouflage, is shown here at Frankfurt. It was later based at the Kwajalein Missile Range and was eventually sold as N9012J and then C9-ATV.

Later Caribous were designated CV-2B and had various improvements including a higher gross weight. Following rationalisation of US Army aviation, the CV-2s were passed on to the USAF, becoming C-7s and this aircraft, 63-9747, seen in September, 1978, wears modern camouflage and AFRES (Air Force Reserve) markings.

The Royal Malaysian Air Force acquired twenty Caribous, the first of them being FM1100 which is shown above at Gatwick Airport in 1966 on delivery. This Caribou was re-serialled FM1401 and then M21-01 and was later sold on the commercial market as N494GA. In Canada, the RCAF obtained six Caribous including the DHC demonstrator, CF-LVA and this aircraft, 5323, (below) which was handed over in November, 1960. These were mainly employed on United Nations support in Cyprus and elsewhere. This Caribou was sold on to Tanzania as JW9015 and was written off in an accident near the Ugandan border.

Zambian Air Force Caribous were delivered in a white and silver colour scheme but several of the five aircraft were later repainted in camouflage. This is the third aircraft, handed over in 1965 and eventually declared surplus in 1984 after being replaced by the Buffalo.

This curious Caribou (63-9737, c/n 182) wears a two-tone blue and white colour scheme and the tail markings of the Mississippi ARNG (Aviation Classification Repair Activity Depot). It is shown here at Pensacola following civilianisation as N6154Y and it later became C-FBOO.

This aircraft, N493GA (c/n 256) was one of three Caribous acquired by Global Associates from DHC for operations at the Kwajalein Missile Range in the Pacific. It was later transferred to the US Army as 66-256 and continued in service at the range, painted in Army colours.

The Royal Australian Air Force continues to use a large fleet of Caribous. They received thirty-one aircraft including A4-159 seen here making a characteristically steep approach to land on its nose-wheel at RAAF Richmond.

The Ugandan Police Air Wing obtained this new Caribou (5X-AAB, c/n 222) from the manufacturers in 1964. Ten years later it was transferred to Uganda Airlines and it was eventually written off in a crash at Entebbe in April 1976.

Tanzania was another African Caribou operator, receiving no fewer than twelve aircraft between 1966 and 1971, six of these being former RCAF aircraft. Their third aircraft, JW9003 (c/n 244), became 5H-AAB and was then sold to John Woods as N1017L. It is seen here in derelict condition outside the NCA hangar at Safi in 1993.

During the 1970s, the Kenya Air Force built up a large aircraft fleet and they acquired six new Caribous to provide logistics support to military bases on the Somali border. The aircraft (above) (c/n 237) was eventually disposed of as N600NC to NCA who sold it to Pen Turbo Aviation for experimental conversion with PT6A turboprop engines. Relatively unpublicised is the batch of five DHC-4 Caribous delivered to the Abu Dhabi Army Air Wing. The first of these was No.301 (c/n 269) (below) handed over in 1969 but this was written of in an accident at Radum on 28 October, 1976.

Spanish Air Force T.9 Caribous were painted in an attractive brown, tan and green camouflage as seen on T9-3, photographed prior to delivery. An initial batch of twelve new aircraft delivered in 1967/68 was joined in 1980 by twenty-four former USAF aircraft. The Spanish Caribou fleet has now been retired and mostly sold to civilian users.

One of the Spanish military aircraft, T9-20, is shown here parked at Malta's Safi Airport carrying the civil registration N56NC prior to delivery by NewCal Aviation (NCA) to Pen Turbo Aviation in June, 1994 as a candidate for modification to turboprop power.

The first of the seven-aircraft batch of Caribous for the Ghana Air Force, G400 (c/n 28), was delivered in November, 1961 and remained in service until July, 1974. Here, it is shown painted in the white, red and yellow colours adopted by the Ghana Air Force, but is registered N90565. It was sold to Pen Turbo Aviation but ended up being scrapped at Cape May, New Jersey.

Officially delivered to Air Asia in July 1962 this Caribou (B-853, c/n 52) carried Civil Air Transport (CAT) of Taiwan titles on its natural metal finish. In reality, Air Asia, CAT, Air America and Pacific Architects & Engineers, who acquired a dozen Caribous, were front organisations for the American CIA's operations in South-East Asia.

Retaining the anonymous natural metal that characterised CIA aircraft, N539Y (c/n 197) was demobilised and acquired by Alaska Air Service in 1977. The Caribou was very popular with freight carriers in Canada and Alaska due to its convenient tail loading ramp, the easily serviced Wasp engines and its high payload. N539Y was later used as a fuel transport and crashed and burned in Alaska in 1986.

Another Caribou seen at Anchorage in the early 1980s was N581PA (c/n 253) used by Sea Airmotive for hauling fish and other commodities and destroyed in a crash at Bullen Point, Alaska in August, 1979. The registration reveals that this is another ex-CIA aircraft originally registered to Pacific Architects & Engineers.

While externally similar in dimensions and appearance to the Caribou, the DHC-5 Buffalo had a substantially enlarged fuselage, a T-tail and General Electric CT64 turboprops. 63-13687 was the second of four evaluation CV-7A Buffaloes built for the US Army in 1965 but a change of policy meant that no production order was placed.

The Ecuadorian Air Force bought two DHC-5D Buffaloes, the second of which was FAE-064 (c/n 64) seen here prior to delivery. This particular aircraft was destroyed in an accident in July 1990 and the other aircraft has also been written off.

With the disappointment of losing a potential US Army order, de Havilland had the consolation of selling the Buffalo to the Canadian Armed Forces. Fifteen CC-115s were delivered including several, such as 115454 (above), in Search and Rescue configuration.

Ten CC-115 Buffaloes of the Canadian Armed forces are seen lined up in the snow at Toronto. These are standard cargo/transport versions and wear full camouflage. By the end of 1999 only six Buffaloes remained in service with the Canadian Armed Forces.

Having been a good customer for the Caribou, the Kenyan Air Force went on to buy an initial batch of six Buffaloes followed by a further four. This factory photo shows the second aircraft that was delivered, serial number 208.

Brazil was a large Buffalo customer, acquiring twenty-four out of the 151 aircraft built. Many were camouflaged but 2359 (c/n 29) seen here is painted in a simple silver and white colour scheme.

A pair of Buffaloes went to Togo to provide logistical support for the Force Aérienne Togolaise. 5V-MAG and 5V-MAH were camouflaged in brown and tan and carried yellow civil prefixed registrations. Both have now been sold to commercial users.

In 1976 the Zaire Air Force (Force Aérienne Zairoise) obtained three new Buffaloes from DHC. Two of these are believed to be still in service with the Air Force of the Democratic Republic of Congo including 9T-CBA.

Ecuador was a customer for two Buffaloes, built in 1976. Both have been reported as having been written off but this aircraft, serialled AEE-501, remains in service and may be a rebuild of one or both of the original airframes.

De Havilland brought Buffalo C-GCTC (c/n 103) into service as a demonstrator in 1979 with the objective of gaining orders for the Transporter civil variant. During a spirited demonstration at the Farnborough Air Show in September 1984 it made a very heavy landing which tore the wings off. Fortunately the rugged Buffalo fuselage survived and the crew walked away.

The fifth Buffalo had an interesting career, initially as 115451 with the RCAF and then as the XC-8A test aircraft for the Bell Air Cushion Landing System. The large air cushion bag was powered by two small turbines seen here fitted under the wing roots and the aircraft also had wingtip floats for water landings.

In another experimental test role, N716NA (C-GFIU) was modified by Boeing for joint Canadian and NASA augmentor wing research. Rebuilt with two (and later, four) Rolls-Royce Spey 801 turbofans, the Buffalo used jet thrust ducted from the engines to special flaps to give dramatically improved STOL performance.

Several US Government agencies have used the Buffalo and this example is the third of the US Army evaluation batch of CV-7As handed over to the US Department of Commerce Environmental Science Services Agency (ESSA) as ESSA-88 for coastal and geodetic survey work.

This Buffalo, carrying the US Navy serial 161546, remains something of a mystery. It carries US Navy titles and the tail markings of the Naval Weapons Center at China Lake although no examples of the Buffalo appear in the US Navy inventory.

In addition to manufacturing its own designs, DHC was contracted to build a batch of Grumman Tracker anti-submarine aircraft for the Royal Canadian Navy. As a pattern aircraft, they received one Grumman-built S2F-1, above, which was serialled 1500.

De Havilland built one hundred CS2F Trackers and this is the first of the second batch of fifty-seven improved CS2F-2 variants that were fitted with Litton tactical navigation systems. Seventeen of the early CS2F-1s were sold to the Royal Netherlands Navy for service in the Netherlands' Antilles.

This CS2F-2 Tracker was delivered with the serial 1548 but was later re-serialled 12148. This photo shows the complex wing folding mechanism that was essential for carrier storage.

Once discarded by the Royal Canadian Navy, several Trackers found a new life as water bombers to combat forest fires on behalf of the Ontario Department of Lands and Forests. They were converted by Field Aviation and later by Conair who also sold several to the French Sécurité Civile as Firecats.

Five

The New Commuter Market

With the Beaver and the Otter, de Havilland Canada gathered a reputation and a faithful following of small air carriers and bush operators. While the Caribou and the Buffalo were designed to meet the needs of air forces and cargo carriers they were not suitable for a new breed of airlines which emerged in the mid-1960s – the Commuter Air Carriers. The DHC-6 Twin Otter started out literally as an Otter with two PT6 turboprop engines and a tricycle undercarriage. However, it soon grew to provide the capacity for twenty passengers that suited the new group of small airlines which started to offer local service from main hub airports to local communities. The US Army again failed to place a substantial order – but de Havilland's production line was already filling up with Twin Otters for Golden West, Pilgrim Airlines and Air Wisconsin. By the time the production line closed, 844 examples of the DHC-6 had left the Downsview factory. DHC's succes with the commuter carriers inevitably brought demands for increased capacity and the four-engined DHC-7, which carried no name but quickly became known as the 'Dash-7', was designed to provide fifty-seat capacity with outstanding STOL ability. This combination allowed the Dash-7 to carry large loads in and out of difficult and noise-sensitive airfields including the city centre 'STOLports' such as London's City Airport. DHC built 113 Dash-7s and these are still much sought after.

The Scottish airline, Loganair, was an enthusiastic user of the Twin Otter which was able to combine respectable cruising performance with the ability to land on the short airfields and sand strips in the north of Scotland. G-BGEN flew for them from 1979 to 1982 and was later sold to Indonesia.

The Canadian Armed Forces purchased nine Twin Otters that were delivered in 1971. The third aircraft, 13803 (c/n 305) shows off the overall yellow colour scheme which was applied to assist its search and rescue role.

This Twin Otter is one of three surviving aircraft out of five acquired by the Royal Norwegian Air Force as general-purpose transports. 67-062 (c/n 62) was handed over in September, 1967 and is a Series 100 with the original short nose.

As with other DHC types, the Twin Otter was expected to fly in all conditions and this picture clearly shows the large floats used on many DHC-6s. C-GKBV (c/n 287), seen here landing at Vancouver, is one of the large fleet of Kenn Borek Air and was used for some time on the company's air taxi operations in the Maldive Islands as 8Q-KBV.

When winter arrives the Twin Otters swap floats for skis. This yellow and black Twin Otter 300, C-FTFX (c/n 340) of Ptarmigan Air sits on a frozen lake in Canada equipped with its ski-only undercarriage. For float operations, later Twin Otters were fitted with the short Series 100 nose for better visibility.

Floatplanes are a vital part of life on the Canadian west coast and West Coast Air is one of the operators flying local services out of Vancouver. This Twin Otter, C-FWCA (c/n 468), has large panoramic cabin windows fitted by its previous owner, Scenic Airlines, for Grand Canyon sightseeing flights.

The Peruvian Air Force purchased nineteen Twin Otters, all of which were capable of operating on floats. The first aircraft, FAP-390 (c/n 73) is pictured over Toronto prior to delivery in 1967. It was later sold back to Canada for use by Pacific Petroleum Ltd.

In 1967 when the commuter airlines boom was developing, Golden West flew a large fleet of Twin Otters including N950SM (c/n 90) seen above at San Francisco. Their fleet of Twin Otters and Dash-7s operated passenger services up and down the California coastal strip. On the East Coast, Pilgrim Airlines was one of the early commuter operators and N121PM (c/n 14) (below) was one of eight Twin Otters used on routes between Boston, Providence, Bridgeport and New York. They were fitted with unusual angled seats to give passengers extra legroom.

Although the US Army preferred the Beech U-21 for utility transport they did buy a number of Twin Otters for more demanding operations. This DHC-6, 76-22565 (c/n 495) is one of eight aircraft designated UV-18A and illustrated in Alaska National Guard markings.

Lambair was a major bush operator in Manitoba and this bright red Twin Otter, CF-AUS (c/n 34), flew with them for thirteen years until it was written off in an accident at Mealy Mountains near Goose Bay in October 1984. It is equipped with an oversize nosewheel for rough field landings.

The Series 200 and 300 Twin Otters had longer noses with additional baggage space; 3X-GAY (c/n 553) is a Series 300 with the higher-powered PT6A-27 engines. It is shown here in service as a mining transport with Compagnie de Bauxites Guinée at its base at Conakry in Equatorial Guinea.

From the days of the Otter, Widerees has been an enthusiastic DHC customer and has flown a succession of Twin Otters on airline services along the Norwegian Fjord coastline. LN-BNS was delivered in March 1977 but was written off on take-off from Vaeroey in the Lofoten Islands in April 1990.

Although painted in Argentine Air Force markings, this Twin Otter 200, T-83 (c/n 170) is one of a fleet of state-owned aircraft used for community transport services within Argentina. Nine Twin Otters were delivered for this purpose from 1968 onwards.

The Argentine Navy obtained one new Twin Otter 200 in February 1969 for work in the Antarctic operating out of Punta Arenas in Tierra del Fuego. This aircraft, 1-G-101 (c/n 171), was on strength from 1969 to 1973 when it was sold to an Argentine commercial company.

Following a proud tradition, the Twin Otter has served with the British Antarctic Survey since 1968 and eight aircraft have been used at various times. They are registered in the Falkland Islands and VP-FBL (c/n 839) was one of the last Twin Otters built.

G-BDHC (c/n 414) was supplied by its sponsor, the Chubb Group, to support the British Transglobe Expedition. Led by Sir Ranulph Fiennes, this expedition longitudinally circled the globe, starting at Greenwich in September 1979 and completing the circle in August, 1982.

The French Armée de l'Air is one of the many military users of the Twin Otter. Nine aircraft have been delivered including No.603 seen awaiting passengers at Le Bourget Airport near Paris.

Large numbers of Twin Otters have been used in Colombia including HK-2821 (c/n 533) operated by Aeroejecutivos for a period in the mid-1980s. It is shown here at Miami Opa Locka in test markings prior to sale to Israel where it operated with Arkia as 4X-AHZ.

Lesotho Airways was one of the many African airlines who found the Twin Otter highly economical and operationally efficient. They had a substantial fleet and eight were operated during the 1980s including 7P-LAB (c/n 623).

Another African user was Air Tanzania whose colourful blue and yellow livery adorns Twin Otter 300, 5H-MRB (c/n 579) taxiing out at its Dar-es-Salaam base. It was delivered in May 1978 and in 1993 was sold to Air Kenya.

The Twin Otter has been used widely for aerial survey work and N999PG (c/n 721) sits in front of the Downsview hangar in test markings following the fitting of its wingtip pads and nose probe for Geosurvey International. It was later transferred to the Australian Geographic Society as VH-SWH.

Another array for survey work is seen here on the early production Twin Otter CF-INB-X (c/n 23) purchased by the Canadian Nickel Co. in 1966 and operated by Survair Ltd. The trailing 'bird' beneath the fuselage is noteworthy. This aircraft later went on to serve with International Nickel in Indonesia.

Based at Silvio Petirossi Airport outside Asuncion, FAP-02 (c/n 137) is one of the Paraguayan Air Force's fleet of governmental transports. It is fitted out with an executive interior and used to transport the Paraguayan President on internal flights.

Taxiing at St Lucia Vigie Airport in the Leeward Islands is one of the eleven Twin Otters flown by Leeward Islands Air Transport at various times over its Caribbean routes. V2-LCK (c/n 762) joined the airline in October, 1982.

The Dash-7 was a completely new design – and a substantially larger aircraft than the Twin Otter with four Pratt & Whitney PT6A-50 turboprops, a retractable tricycle undercarriage and a T-tail. The prototype, C-GNBX made its first flight on 27 March 1975 and is now preserved at the Canadian National Aviation Museum at Rockliffe.

Rocky Mountain Airways was the launch customer for the Dash-7, receiving their first aircraft N27RM in November 1977. They specialised in serving skiers arriving at Denver who needed to go on to the Colorado ski resorts of Vail and Aspen.

Canadian Armed Forces Squadron 412 operated a pair of Dash-7s (CC-132s) from Lahr Air Force Base in Germany. The first aircraft, 132001 (c/n 8) was fitted with a VIP interior.

Air Wisconsin developed a very successful Dash-7 service out of Chicago to Appleton in southern Wisconsin. Shown here is N890S (c/n 13) delivered in July 1979.

In England, Brymon Airways acquired Dash-7s to serve routes from London to West Country airports such as Plymouth and Newquay. G-BRYA (c/n 062) is seen here after Brymon was acquired by British Airways.

Arkia became one of the largest Dash-7 operators with thirteen being flown at various times. In this photo taken at Eilat, 4X-AHJ (c/n 050) takes off on a scheduled flight to Jerusalem.

Several of the Arkia Dash-7s were painted in sponsored colour schemes. One aircraft carried a livery representing the VISA credit card organisation and this aircraft, 4X-AHC (c/n 082) has a yellow, orange and green fish painted on the side to advertise Club Hotel.

The Dash-7 must take much of the credit for the success of the London City Airport that had demanding noise and approach profiles. One of the last production aircraft, G-BOAX (c/n 111), was used between 1988 and 1990 by Eurocity Express to serve Paris and Brussels, painted with a pinstripe business suit tail logo.

For short-haul inter-island services, the Dash-7 was an ideal aircraft for Hawaiian Airlines. One of their aircraft in two-tone pink livery waits a new passenger load in September 1989 at Honolulu International Airport.

Standing on the tarmac at Sendre Stromfjord is OY-CBU, one of the Dash-7s used by Groenlandsfly to provide a scheduled service between the capital of Greenland, Godthab and other towns such as Narssarssuaq and Kulusuk.

Emirates Air Service used this Dash-7, A6-ALM to fly scheduled and charter services out of Abu Dhabi to other airports in the Persian Gulf area.

Berjaya Air acquired this Dash-7, 9M-TAL in November 1995 from Brymon Air and until recently it flew services out of Kuala Lumpur's Subang Airport, where it is seen here.

Six
Regional Aircraft

As the 1970s drew to a close, de Havilland Canada was strongly positioned in the Commuter Airline market with the twenty-seat Twin Otter and fifty-seat Dash-7. It was clear that there was a need for an 'in-between' airliner providing between twenty-five and forty-five seats and this emerged as the DHC-8 'Dash-8' which made its maiden flight on 20 June 1983. Following the now-familiar high wing that had become the company's design trademark, the Dash-8 had a tall T-tail and was powered by new Pratt & Whitney PW120 turboprops. Despite difficult conditions for the commuter airlines, orders started to accumulate and the Dash-8 found an expanding market for regional airliners serving routes of up to two hours duration. Not surprisingly, growing passenger demand in this sector resulted in new requests for the larger Dash-7, but it was clear that a stretched Dash-8 made manufacturing sense for DHC, and its twin-engined economy would benefit the customer. The new fifty-six-passenger Dash-8-300 soon found a ready market and the call for still greater capacity prompted an even larger stretch to produce the Dash-8-400. This first flew in January 1998. With the introduction of new vibration and noise suppression 'Quiet Technology' and a range of three cabin sizes, de Havilland Canada, now a part of Bombardier, has taken a dominant position in the turboprop airliner sector and had sold over 600 of the Dash-8 series by the end of 2000.

Down in the Caribbean, Leeward Islands Air Transport has been a major customer for the Dash-8. Awaiting passengers at St Lucia is V2-LCZ (c/n 048), a Dash-8-100 delivered in September, 1986.

With modern computer design tools and pre-prototype research de Havilland Canada was able to ensure that the flying prototype of the Dash-8 was virtually in production configuration. Here a Dash-8 model is readied for wind tunnel testing.

The Dash-8 prototype, C-GDNK approaches to land at Downsview in 1983. This aircraft went on to become the stretched Dash-8-300 prototype and was finally broken up in March 1990.

Air Canada's local service network became a major customer for the Dash-8. This picture taken at Downsview shows C-G JIG (c/n 68), a Dash-8-100 of Air Ontario which operates a network of routes in the Toronto area.

This picture of the interior of an early Dash-8-100 clearly illustrates the deep stand-up cabin of the aircraft and the careful attention to hand baggage stowage in the contoured overhead lockers.

A Dash-8-100, C-GGTO (c/n 005) of City Express, passes the eastern suburbs of Toronto en route to Montreal. The airline used a mixed fleet of Dash-7s and Dash-8s linking Toronto's Island Airport with Ottawa and Montreal at a frequency of up to eight flights daily.

The Dash-8 was used by Metro Airlines in association with Eastern Airlines to link cities along the Atlantic coast from New York to Florida. N804MX (c/n 019) is seen in full Eastern Metro Express livery prior to the collapse of Eastern Airlines in January, 1991.

During the 1990s, many of the United States trunk carriers formed syndicated feeder subsidiaries to serve small communities from the main hubs. US Air Express operators included Allegeheny, Piedmont and CC Air; this leased Series 100, C-GTAF (c/n 083) is seen in the original US Air colour scheme at Tampa, Florida.

US Air changed their colour scheme to a predominantly black upper fuselage and tail with red and white trim and a stylised American flag on the fin. At the end of 2000, there were over 130 Dash-8s in use by US Air Express operators including N833EX (c/n 282) of Allegheny Airlines.

By the end of 2000 de Havilland Canada had delivered nearly 170 Dash-8-300s. This picture shows a new Series 300 for the Chinese Zhejiang Airlines in the final assembly process at Downsview in 1989.

British Columbia was served by another of the Air Canada regional subsidiaries – Air BC. This aircraft, C-FADJ (c/n 322) is a Series 100 and wears the later Air Canada colour scheme with a red maple leaf on a dark green tail.

This Southern Australia Airlines Dash-8-100, VH-WZJ (c/n 021), wears the livery of its parent company, Australian Airlines (formerly TAA). It is seen here at Melbourne Tullamarine in 1992 prior to the merger of Australian Airlines and Qantas.

Following the Qantas-Australian merger in November 1993 the Australian fleet was repainted in the red and white Qantas colours. VH-WZJ is seen again in its new livery at Sydney Airport in May 1996.

D-BIRT is a Dash-8 Series 103A, operated by Augsburg Airways and seen above taxiing in at Frankfurt in August 1998. The airline was formed in 1980 as Interot Airways and it is now part of the Team Lufthansa alliance and flies fourteen Dash-8s. The Dash-8 Series 200 was an improved Series 100 with higher-powered PW123C engines and an increased useful load. This Series 200 (below), 9M-EKB (c/n 418), had a brief career with the Malaysian operator, Saeaga Airlines in 1996/97.

The USAF, which is among a number of military Dash-8 operators, uses a pair of E-9As, including 84-0048 (c/n 045) shown here. These are fitted with a large fuselage fairing to house a phased array antenna for tracking and information relay at the Gulf Coast Missile Test Range.

Six CT-142s have been supplied to the Canadian Armed Forces. These are Series 100 Dash-8s; 142805 (c/n 103) is fitted with an extended radar nose and used as a navigation trainer.

Founded in 1981, Horizon Air is one of the principal regional airlines in the Pacific Northwest and is a subsidiary of Alaska Airlines. It operates out of Seattle and at the end of 2000 was one of the largest Dash-8 operators with forty-two aircraft including N811PH (c/n 023) shown here in its early colour scheme.

Southern Winds is a regional airline providing service in Argentina from Buenos Aires to Mendoza, Bahia Blanca and Cordoba with six Dash-8-100s. LV-ZGB (c/n 364) is shown taxiing out at Buenos Aires Aeroparque Airport in March, 2000.

While the Dash-8 range was expanding to meet the needs of growing airlines, there was a market niche in the twenty-five seat category. In 1986, de Havilland Canada and Shorts joined in a new study that resulted in the NRA.90-A. The model above shows a close family resemblance to the Dash-8.

The NR.90-B was a more radical design, still with twenty-five seats in three-abreast layout but with the twin turbine engines buried in the rear fuselage driving two counter-rotating pusher propellers in the tail. In the event, neither of the NRA designs went into production.

Serving destinations in the Arabian Gulf, A6-ADA (c/n 471) is one of a pair of Dash-8-Q-200s acquired from the manufacturers by Abu Dhabi Aviation in May, 1997. Lufthansa Cityline is one of the largest regional airlines in Europe and has partnerships with several airlines including Contact Air. Their Dash-8-300, D-BKIM (c/n 356) (below) was photographed in 1993 prior to delivery at Downsview in full Lufthansa livery.

Named *City of Palmerston North*, ZK-NES (c/n 125) is the first of four Dash-8-102s acquired by Ansett New Zealand. Seen here at Auckland Airport, it was originally delivered to Great China Airlines in 1988.

The Dash-8-300 addressed the demand for a fifty-seat capacity aircraft and one of the early customers was Hamburg Airlines who received D-BOBS (c/n 342) in December, 1992. It was used on European routes from Hamburg to London, Antwerp, Gothenburg and Rotterdam.

Following its acquisition by British Airways in 1993 Brymon Airways' fleet of Dash-8s was repainted in British Airways Express livery. One of their seventeen-strong fleet of Series 300 aircraft, G-BRYK (c/n 284), awaits its passenger load at Paris Charles de Gaulle in July 1998.

Another of the Brymon fleet of Dash-8-300s is G-BRYT (c/n 334) in the new World Image colour scheme launched by British Airways in June 1997. The tail on G-BRYT is the sole example of the 'Colour Down the Side' design devised by Terry Frost.

Wearing the minimalist colour scheme of SABENA, PH-SDM (c/n 298) is one of five Dash-8-300s, which were operated by Schreiner Airways on SABENA's low density short haul European feeder routes.

Making a steep approach to land at the 1998 Farnborough Air Show is the stylishly decorated DHC demonstrator Dash-8-Q300. The new Q-Series features a Noise and Vibration Suppression System that compensates for structural vibration and results in exceptional passenger comfort.

With a fuselage stretch of 22.2ft compared with the Dash-8-300, the seventy-five-seat Series Q400 must be the ultimate Dash-8 development. The second prototype, C-GCLI (c/n 4002), is shown above on take-off from Dorval. By November 2000, Bombardier Regional Aircraft had logged sixty-eight orders for the Q400. Below is the company demonstrator, C-GIHK, painted with the unusual flower design in light blue. The additional tail bullet fairing of the Q400 can be seen clearly in this photograph.

Horizon Air is to receive fifteen Q400s to add to an existing fleet of 49 Series 100/200 aircraft. The current Horizon colour scheme can be compared with the original orange trim seen on the aircraft on page 120.

SAS Commuter was the first European airline to receive the Q400 and twenty-eight have been ordered to fill the capacity gap between the SAS Fokker 50s and their fleet of Boeing 737s and MD.80s. This photograph emphasises the exceptional length of the Q400 fuselage.

The Taiwan-based Uni Air is part of the EVA Airways group and has operated a fleet of twelve Dash-8-300s since it began operations under the name Great China Airways in 1989. Its latest purchase is six Q400s, one of which is seen above.

Already a good Dash-8 Customer, the Austrian carrier Tyrolean is in the course of receiving six Q400s. The wing of the Q400 is slightly longer than the Q300, which allows the engine nacelles and propellers greater clearance from the fuselage and further improves cabin noise levels.